# George Washington

## By Kathie Billingslea Smith
### Illustrated by James Seward

Julian Messner
New York

Cover Portrait: Sam Patrick

Copyright © 1987 by Ottenheimer Publishers, Inc. All rights reserved including the right of reproduction in whole or in part in any form. Published by JULIAN MESSNER, A Division of Simon & Schuster, Inc., Simon & Schuster Building, Rockefeller Center, 1230 Avenue of the Americas, New York, New York 10020. JULIAN MESSNER and colophon are trademarks of Simon & Schuster, Inc.
Printed in U.S.A.

**Library of Congress Cataloging-in-Publication Data**

Smith, Kathie Billingslea.
George Washington

(Great Americans)
"A Wanderer book."
Summary: A biography of our first President with illustrations that are reproductions of paintings, documents, and photographs from the Smithsonian and National Gallery.
1. Washington, George, 1732-1799—Juvenile literature. 2. Presidents—United States—Biography—Juvenile literature. [1. Washington, George, 1732-1799. 2. Presidents] I. Title. II. Series: Great Americans (New York, N.Y.)
E312.66.S65  1987  973.3'092'4  [B]  [92]  86-28064
ISBN 0-671-64147-6

Courtesy of the Library of Congress, Washington D.C.

George Washington was born in a small brick house on a plantation on the Virginia side of the Potomac River. His actual birthdate was February 11, 1732. In later years the calendar was changed, and eleven days were added to correct a past mistake. George's birthday then became February 22nd, but he always preferred to celebrate it on February 11th.

George's parents, Augustine and Mary Ball Washington, lived comfortably. George was their first child, but he soon had many brothers and sisters.

Not much is known about his childhood. It is believed that he attended school in Fredericksburg. He loved to count and measure things, and was very good at mathematics.

On the three family plantations, George often helped his father and older half-brothers from his father's first marriage, Augustine Jr. and Lawrence. George became a fine horseman and could shoot and ride extremely well.

When George was eleven years old, his father died. The family plantations were willed, one each, to Augustine Jr., Lawrence, and George. Lawrence renamed his plantation "Mount Vernon" in honor of his past commander in the British Royal Navy, Admiral Edward Vernon.

Lawrence was a great friend and influence over George. By his mid-teens, George was living at Mount Vernon with Lawrence and his wife Anne.

◀ George Washington as a Virginia lieutenant colonel.

George became interested in surveying and drawing maps. He was soon working as a county surveyor. He helped to lay out the new town of Alexandria, just across the Potomac River from the spot where a city would one day be named for him. With his earnings, George bought 2,000 acres of land in the Shenandoah Valley.

In 1752, Lawrence died of tuberculosis. George inherited his estate, which included Mount Vernon. At the age of twenty, he found himself in charge of two plantations and a large parcel of unsettled land.

▲ Mount Vernon as it looks today.

In 1754, the Governor of Virginia made George Washington lieutenant colonel of a troop of Virginians and sent them to the Ohio River Valley to claim the land for Britain. The Virginians were involved in several battles with the French and the Indians. George was excited by the challenge of war. A newspaper quoted him as saying, "I heard the bullets whistle, and, believe me, there is something charming in the sound.

The struggle for land in the Ohio River Valley lasted for seven years and became known as the French and Indian War. Washington was a clever soldier and was made Commander-in-Chief of the Virginia Forces.

Courtesy of the Library of Congress, Washington D.C.

After several years of fighting, Washington gave up
the life of a soldier and returned to his farms at Mount
Vernon. In 1759, at the age of twenty-six, he married
Martha Custis, a wealthy widow with two children, Patsy and Jack.
George was a good father and husband, and raised the two children as
his own.

Mount Vernon, like most other big plantations, had a large staff of
workers and slaves. They raised almost all of their own food and made
their own clothing and shoes. Washington was a hard-working farmer.
He grew wheat and built a mill to make flour. He also caught a great
number of herring in the Potomac River and sold them, salted, in
barrels.

George and Martha had a happy family life. They attended church regularly and helped to look after the poor people of the parish. For entertainment they went to dances and played card games of whist and loo with their friends and neighbors. George loved to ride his horses and was an accomplished equestrian.

Several times, George was elected to the house of Burgesses. He quickly learned the workings of government. He was a handsome man—6'2" tall, with dark hair and bluish gray eyes—and was well-known throughout the colony of Virginia.

Courtesy of the Library of Congress, Washington D.C.

In 1763 the French and Indian War ended. Britain was the victor and gained Canada and territories west of the colonies.

The war had cost Britain a lot of money. King George III of England decided to make the colonists in America pay more money in taxes. The colonists were very angry about this. Washington wrote to a friend, "I think the Parliament of Great Britain hath no more right to put their hands into my pocket, without my consent, than I have to put my hands in yours for money."

In 1769, he introduced a set of resolves in the Virginia House of Burgesses, declaring that the colonies had the right to tax themselves.

▶ King George III of Great Britain

The Second Continental Congress voting independence.

The British Parliament sent soldiers to police the angry colonists in Boston and closed that port city. George Washington and others angrily protested these actions. Then the British Governor disbanded the Virginia Assembly. The colonists knew that something had to be done to decide the separate rights and powers of the colonies and Britain.

Colonists from twelve of the thirteen colonies held a special meeting, known as the First Continental Congress, in Philadelphia in 1774. Washington was one of seven delegates representing Virginia. The delegates voted to stop buying supplies from Britain and to meet again in May of 1775. In every colony, men began to practice military drills, and gather weapons.

Courtesy of the National Archives, Washington, D.C.

For more than one hundred years, the colonies had developed and grown stronger. Now they wanted to govern themselves. They did not want Britain to tell them what to do. "Is it the interest of a man to be a boy all his life?" questioned a colonist named Thomas Paine.

But Britain was not ready to give up the colonies.

In Lexington and Concord, Massachusetts, British soldiers shot and killed some of the colonists there. These "shots heard 'round the world" were the beginning of the Revolutionary War.

All thirteen colonies were represented at the Second Continental Congress. They were determined to defend themselves against the British troops. On June 15, 1775, the delegates unanimously elected George Washington to be general and Commander-in-Chief of the Continental Army. Washington accepted the post and insisted on receiving no salary for his work.

He left immediately for Massachusetts to help the "Sons of Liberty" there organize an army. In a letter to Martha at Mount Vernon, he wrote about his love for her and said that he would probably be home in the fall. Little did he know that the war would drag on for more than six years.

◄ John Hancock presenting commission to George Washington as Commander-in-Chief of the Continental Army.

JOHN HANCOCK PRESENTING COMMISSION TO GEORGE WASHINGTON

In Congress

To George Washington Esquire

FAC-SIMILE OF THE COMMISSION

Courtesy of the Library of Congress, Washington, D.C.

Courtesy of the National Archives, Washington D.C.

When Washington arrived in Massachusetts, he found an army made up of untrained farmers, hunters, and businessmen. They wore whatever clothes were handy. Soon they were joined by forces from Maryland, Pennsylvania, and Virginia. These men wore fringed hunting shirts and were excellent marksmen with their long barreled rifles.

The British soldiers, part of a trained army, wore dressy uniforms of bright red and looked down on the colonial soldiers.

"The redcoats do look the best," Washington stated, "but it takes the ragged boys to do the fighting."

Washington and his men forced the British troops to abandon Boston, leaving the city free once again. But the war was just getting started.

A large fleet of British ships sailed into the New York harbor on July 2, 1776. This was the same day that the Second Continental Congress was voting to approve the Declaration of Independence. Thousands of British soldiers and many hired German soldiers, known as mercenaries, joined the British forces in New Jersey and New York.

With fewer supplies and fewer men, Washington's army was forced to go south. They rowed across the icy Delaware River to New Jersey on Christmas night of 1776. The next morning they launched a successful surprise attack on a camp of German mercenaries at Trenton. In forty-five minutes, more than 900 Germans were killed or captured. Only four of Washington's men died, two of whom froze to death.

In the fall of 1777, other British troops sailed up the Chesapeake Bay and marched to Philadelphia. Washington's smaller army could not keep them out, and the British settled in there for the winter.

The Continental army was forced to camp nearby on a cold, windy plateau in Valley Forge. It was a dreadful winter. Thousands of men died from typhus, smallpox, and dysentery. There was little food, and many men deserted and went home. Washington earned his soldiers' respect by living as they did, with no extra luxuries. A visit from Martha cheered him considerably. At winter's end, only 3,000 of his original 11,000 soldiers were left at the camp.

Courtesy of the Library of Congress, Washington D.C.

▲ Washington taking command of the Continental Army.

In the spring of 1778 France decided to help the colonists in their fight for independence. France declared war on Britain and sent soldiers and supplies to the colonies. Washington was thrilled. Britain now had two wars to fight and could not give her full attention to America.

Washington and his troops continued to fight, winning some battles and losing others. By April of 1781, Washington's spirits were low. He ached to see his home and family again. When reminded that he had once found charm in the whistling of bullets, Washington replied, "If I said so, it was when I was young."

Washington learned that a large troop of British soldiers, under General Cornwallis, was camped at Yorktown, Virginia, waiting for British ships to pick them up and go north. Immediately Washington went south to New Jersey. There he built a dummy encampment to make it look as if his troops were settling in for awhile. But then he quickly left the camp behind and traveled down the Chesapeake Bay to Williamsburg, Virginia. The British ships that hoped to link up with Cornwallis' men were chased away by a French fleet. Washington's troops, 17,000 strong, surrounded Yorktown. On October 17, 1781, Cornwallis called for a truce to end the fightng.

Then the British surrendered to Washington. After six long years of fighting, the war was over! Washington had taken a motley band of colonials in Boston and formed an army that had changed history.

When Washington bid goodbye to the army officers who had served under him for so many years, he was choked with emotion and could not bear to speak. With tears streaming down his face, he silently hugged each one.

Two years later on September 3, 1783, a formal peace treaty was signed in Paris. America was now free and independent! The country included land from the Great Lakes to Florida, and from the Atlantic Ocean to the Mississippi River.

As Washington traveled back to Mount Vernon, church bells rang and guns fired in salute to him. He arrived home to greet Martha on Christmas Eve, 1783. He was fifty years old and wanted to spend the rest of his days at this place that he loved best of all.

In his absence, Mount Vernon had become quite run down. Washington busied himself with repairs and new projects. High atop his house he mounted a new weathervane. It was a dove with an olive branch of peace in its beak.

During the war, Martha's children, Patsy and Jack, had both died. George and Martha adopted two of Jack's children and brought them to live at Mount Vernon.

Courtesy of the National Archives, Washington D.C.

THE FOUNDATION OF AMERICAN GOVERNMENT

The thirteen American colonies were now free, but they were not united. Each state had the power to make its own decisions. Disagreements between the states were common. Ben Franklin noted that it was very hard to "make thirteen clocks strike as one."

In May of 1787, a gathering was held in Philadelphia to write a new Constitution and set up one new government for all the states. George Washington was a delegate from Virginia and was elected president of the convention.

After weeks of study and debate, a new form of democratic government—the one that we still use today—was agreed upon.

The new Constitution was ratified, or accepted, by nine of the thirteen states in June of 1788. George Washington was unanimously elected to be the first President of the United States, with John Adams of Massachusetts as Vice-President.

Washington took his oath of office on April 30, 1789, in New York City, which was then the nation's capital. He was dressed in a brown suit made of cloth woven in Connecticut. From that point on, Washington always wore clothes manufactured in America.

Shortly after the inauguration, George and Martha visited every state in the nation. They tried very hard to make the colonists feel that they were all Americans and part of one country.

▼ Vice-President John Adams.

In September of 1790, the capital was moved to Philadelphia and remained there for ten years. Plans were drawn up to build a new capital city near Georgetown, on the Potomac River.

As President of the United States, Washington received a salary of $25,000 per year. This was a very generous income in the late 1700's. His Secretary of State, Thomas Jefferson, and Treasury Secretary, Alexander Hamilton, each received an annual salary of $3,500. Members of Congress were paid $6 per day.

Washington was unanimously elected to serve a second term as President of the United States. He was inaugurated, with John Adams again as Vice-President, on March 4, 1793.

▼ Washington and his cabinet.

During Washington's second term, three new states were admitted to the Union. Vermont joined in 1791, Kentucky in 1792, and Tennessee in 1793.

In 1796, a portrait of Washington was painted by Gilbert Stuart. Today that portrait hangs in the White House in Washington, D.C..

At the end of his second term, Washington decided to retire from the Presidency. He had shepherded the United States through its first rocky years and had helped the new country develop a sense of unity. But now he wanted to go home. He and Martha happily went back to Mount Vernon in March of 1797. John Adams was elected to be the new President, with Thomas Jefferson as Vice-President.

Washington spent his last years at Mount Vernon, overseeing his farms, entertaining visitors, and staying fairly active. He especially enjoyed time spent with his step-grandchildren, Nelly and George Washington Custis.

On December 12, 1799, Washington rode on horseback around his plantations. That night he developed chills and a sore throat. Soon he had trouble breathing. He died on the night of December 14, 1799, at the age of sixty-seven.

In July of 1799, Washington had written a twenty-eight page will. One provision in the will ordered that his slaves, all of whom had been treated kindly, be freed upon his and his wife's deaths.

Washington's funeral was a simple one. He was buried in the family vault at Mount Vernon. People all over the world mourned his passing.

Today Washington's name lives on in many places. Our capital city, one state, seven mountains, ten lakes, thirty-three counties, nine American colleges, 121 towns, and countless streets all bear his name. His picture appears on every nickel, quarter and one-dollar bill.

Throughout his life, Washington was repeatedly asked to help his country and to lead others. He always said "yes" and did his best. Henry Lee said that his good friend George Washington was, "First in war, first in peace, and first in the hearts of his countrymen."